This book belongs to . . . .
School . . . .
Town . . . .
Country . . . .
Planet . . . .
Galaxy . . . .

globular
cluster

hello

remember to
return school
hamster

School

This book is dedicated to
Sally, Claire, Ian, Gail, Sue, Sally
and schoolkids everywhere.

First published in Great Britain by
HarperCollins Publishers Ltd in 1994
10 9 8 7 6 5 4 3 2 1
Text and illustrations copyright
© Colin & Jacqui Hawkins 1994
A CIP catalogue record for this title
is available from the British Library.
The authors assert the moral right to be
identified as the authors of the work.
ISBN: 0 00 193857-6
Printed and bound in Hong Kong
This book is set in Caslon 540 12/15

School

By Colin and Jacqui Hawkins.

Collins

An Imprint of HarperCollinsPublishers

Kids (Types)

Bully Joke:
How do bullies learn to get
what they want?
By trial and terror.

Bully

Thick stupid kid who goes round beating up little or soft kids. Has no real friends, only toadies (see Toadies). Bullies do not like being stared at so try not to look at them. Bullies usually have Whopper or Stinker put before their name, like Stinker Smith or Whopper Wilson. To get even with a bully, put "Kick me Hard" on paper on his/her back.

> **School Proverb**
> Laugh and the school laughs with you.
> Laugh at the school bully and you laugh alone.

> Gimme those sweets or I'll bash you.

Typical bully greeting

Note this is a girl bully, boy bullies are just as ugly

...I won't tell

Toadie

A toadie is someone who sneaks or blabs to teacher. Also called a spoilsport, slimy snake, rat or telltale. Never, never trust a toadie.

> Tell tale tit
> Your tongue will be split
> And all the dogs in town
> Shall have a little bit.

Blabbermouth

Someone who can't keep their gob (mouth) shut. Teller of secrets (see Toadie, see Creep, see Sneak).

> Sneak, baby-sneak
> Your pants do leak!

A friend in need...is a pest.

Are You a Teacher's Pet?

Check out the following; how do you score?

Five points for every YES answered.

Do you have..?

Brain that likes Latin, Algebra, Trigonometry, Geometry.

Alert, clear eyes

Hair neatly combed and brushed (no nits)

Clean inside ears (no potatoes)

Clean behind ears

Face, clean and shiny. (No zits or snot)

Clean neck

Tie always neatly knotted

Clean cuffs

Clean shirt (ironed)

No ink on fingers

Clean fingernails

Apple for teacher

Bag full of finished homework (All neat and tidy. No blots)

Short trousers

Clean knees with no bumps or bruises.

Socks pulled up

Shoelaces done up.

No mud on shoes. Sensible type (No trainers)

Clean, shiny shoes

I'm a teacher's pet.

SCORE:

80-100	Super Teacher's Pet
60-80	Teacher's Pet
40-60	Form Prefect Type
20-40	Nearly a Goodie
5-20	Toadie Type
Zero and below	Average Kid

* Note: clean page (Ed)

Joke to Teacher's Pet

Are you a P.L.P.?

No!

You're quite right.

You're not a proper looking person.

Why is that boy in a cage? Because he's Teacher's pet.

Creep

Kid who says really crawly, cringy, squirmy, wormy things to teachers. (Yuk!)

?

Sir, Sir, I just... wanted to say what a really excellent Math lesson that was, Sir.

Terrible Twittish Jokes

Can a shoe box?
No, but a tin can.

Why do Twits eat biscuits?

Because they're c r a c k e r s.

Twit

Someone who is daft, loco, cracked, barmy, batty or dopey. Not all there.

Twit Quips

You're daft and dithering,
Wipe your chin and stop dribbling.

You're daft, you're potty,
You're made of treacle toffee!

I'm all here

If your nan wets.
There's a big drip under it.

Jelly baby

Crybaby

Kids who weep are called crybabies, diddums, snivellers, blubber-mouths or sissies.

Advice to crybabies:
Go back to your bottle.
Don't make it wet on a dry day.

Baby Bawlings

Crybaby, cry
Put your finger in your eye
Hang him on a lamppost
And leave him there to dry.

Hay is for horses
Straw is for cows
Milk is for babies
That cry out loud

Goody-Goody (Prefect *Perfect)

* Perfect kids, goody-goodies and swots make perfect prefects.

These kids are rarely seen in school. But if you spot one they will have rings of light (halo) over their heads like angels or baby Jesus.

Goody giggle:
What did the cannibal say when he saw Santa Claus?
Goody, goody, Christmas dinner.

I'm a high flier

What floats in space and smells of old kippers?
A nasteroid

Halo – word angels use to greet each other.

Angel

Someone who has wings and flies around in a long white dress. Only seen at school around Christmas time showing sheep and shepherds where baby Jesus is.

I'm as good as gold

Goody-goodies usually win lots of prizes.

Please Sir, I feel a bit strange

Weird Joke: Why did Cyclops give up teaching? Because he only had one pupil.

Weird Kids ——————→

Weird kids are strange and spooky. They like cabbage, wear odd socks, and frequently get lost. Watch out, some teachers are also weird. (Check socks)

tentacle smudge

Weird kids can read upside down.

Evil Kids

Evil kids have power to make you do things that you don't want to do. These are the troublemakers who never get blamed. Look for a 666 on the back of the head, especially if they are called Damien.

Evil Joke: What is Satan's favourite dessert? Devil's Food cake.

I'm lost again

Give me your sticky bun... Give me your sticky bun...

Why was the corpse absent from school? Because he was feeling rotten

?

666

I feel dead on my feet

Dunce

In the olden days (when teacher was young) any kid that didn't know his lessons was called a dunce. He was made to wear a dunce's hat and stand in a corner until he knew the answers. (This could take a long time.)

D

Dunce Ditty
Dunce Dunce double D
Cannot learn his ABC.
Put a cap on, then you'll see
What a silly boy is he.

What a beautiful mourning

Any body there?

Zombies

These are the kids who stay up all night watching TV. They have a deadpan expression and move very slowly.

Do you think zombies enjoy being dead? Of corpse they do.

Foolscap ~ a hat with a large D on it.

Casper's Gags

...s not the cough that
...carries you off.
...s the coffin they
...ry you off in.

It isn't a joke.
Kids that smoke
CROAK!

No if's or butts about it.
You **will** die.

Smokers

Stupid kids think smoking is cool but spend a lot of
time going green and feeling sick. They also get
brown teeth, brown fingers, they never grow,
and they die. Smoking is usually done in the bogs
or behind the bike-sheds.

I know
it all

Vulcan

Big-eared character
from Star Trek.
Rarely seen at school.
Also a know-all.

What illness did
everyone on the
Enterprise catch?
Chicken Spocks.

OTHER TYPES

SNEAK Kid who blabs to
teacher (see Toadie).

WHIZZ KID Someone who is
top of the class. (Usually teacher's pet).

CLEVERDICK Smart, brainy kid.

COPY-CAT A kid who imitates.
Copy-cat, stole a rat.
Put it in his Sunday hat.

CRIBBER Someone who copies
someone else's work.

NOSY PARKER Also known
as Flap-ears, Keyhole Kate.
ANSWER THEIR QUESTIONS WITH:
i) Nosy parker, squashed tomato.
ii) Quizzy flies never grow wise.
iii) Ask no questions and you'll
be told no lies.

SWOT A kid who works hard.

COWARDY-CUSTARD Any kid
who will not take part in a dare.
Also called a Yellow Belly or
Scaredy-Cat.
Cowardy-cowardy custard
Yellow as mustard.

Lessons and Learning

Please God, don't let her ask me...

I kno
Miss

Hands Up

This is what happens when teacher asks a question in class like, "What's the square root of 14 trillion and thirty one?". The kids that know the answer go "Sir! Sir! I know Sir!" and put their hands up. The kids that don't know look stupid and worried, so cruel teachers always ask them. Remember, even if you don't know the answer, put up your hand and go "Sir! Sir! I know Sir!" and wave it about a lot. Teachers never ask kids who know the answer, or appear to know.

Lessons are a cruel rotten way to spend the best days of your life.

Lesson Lore

1. Always be on time for class. Teachers hate late learners.
2. Ignore stupid kids when they pull silly faces at you behind Teacher's back.
3. Teachers hate giggling, gurgling, tittering, hooting, sniggering, chortling, chuckling, and smirking.
4. Never forget your homework.
5. Don't (TO EVERYTHING)

I think that clock is going backwards

Absent

This is when someone is not here, or away, or missing from school (see Sick Note and Diseases). Some kids and some teachers are absent in the mind. If your name is Sharon and teacher calls you George, teacher's mind has gone absent.

Recommended Reading:
Last Day of School by Gladys Friday

Absence makes the heart grow fonder ♡

Clock Watching

School clocks move extremely slowly in lesson time. Try not to watch them as this slows them down even more.

Harry left school with regret. He was sorry he ever had to go.

Silly Snigger: I can't believe you told everyone I was stupid. I'm sorry I didn't realise it was a secret.

Normal kid's brain

Bully brain (pea-brain)

Swot (Mega brain)

??

. . . .

I know, Sir!

Brains

Brains are what you use for school work. The bigger your brain the better you are at knowing the answers to the things teachers ask you.

What happened to the silly bookworm? It died in a brick.

Swot's jot

You Clot!
Why Sir? what?
This blot.
It's snot!

X mark

Mark that looks like a kiss. If your work comes back with lots of x's this does not mean that teacher's in love with you. This is not a kiss. This means your work is wrong.

See me!

Teachers usually put **See Me!** when you get everything wrong.

Look! I got zero.

Brill!

Wow!

Zero

Zilch. Nothing. No mark. Lowest score you can get in a school test. Really wicked (cool). But teachers, mums and dads not impressed.

Teacher's Teaser: Spot the delibrate spelling mistake on this page.

Kid "napping" (dozing, kipping, snoozing)

Kipper: Someone who spends a lot of time sleeping.

Sudden desperate need to go to sleep during lesson time – usually at around three o'clock in the afternoon. Some kids are really good at napping and can "nap" for the whole of a lesson without ever being discovered. Teachers hate nappers and will rudely shout and wake up any kids they see peacefully asleep.

What a thought!
You go to school till you're sixteen. Teachers stay at school until they are SIXTY!

The yawn
Eyes become very heavy.

Pupil: I'm sorry I'm late, Sir, I overslept.
Teacher: You mean you sleep at home as well!

Blatant napping
This is risky, teachers will notice.

Head sinks slowly onto the desk.

Aardvark: rarely seen at school and it makes you very tired

Book keeps out daylight

More subtle napping
Desk lid muffles snores

The book studying method

The head in desk method

Multipliers

two teachers? When he's beside himself

Napper's Rap

Sleepin's a thing I like to do.
It's better than grammar
and two plus two.
I shut my books, I close my eyes.
And dream of burgers, shakes and fries!

What do you call someone who has a dictionary in their wellies?
Smarty boots.

* Cat nap is a brief sleep.

rude remark

YOU LAZY SLUG !!

EEK!

The rude awakening

Horror of Horrors ~ Homework !

All homework and no play can seriously affect your brain.

rrrgh! Cruel idea invented y mean teachers. After a ong hard day at school they jive you **more** work to lug nome. Gross! Mega Gross!

Homework Hints

Avoid doing written homework on the bus. Teachers always recognise "bus shake". Do not copy swot's homework exactly; make a few creative mistakes, otherwise teachers will "suss".

What did you answer for Latin homework, Dimble?

??? .... HOMEWORK??? ARRGH!!! I've not done my homework!!

Swot's perfectly everything right homework.

← 8.45 School Bus just arriving at school gates.

A school kid's work is never done, especially if you forget it!

Horror!

This is the terrible sinking feeling you get when you remember that you've forgotten to do your homework.

Hard Labour

After a long day's toil at school, poor kids struggle home with a typical night's homework: Double Maths, Double Geography, Triple Latin and French irregular verbs.

WARNING

Homework is seriously accident prone. Everything and anything can happen to homework. It will get lost, it will get thrown in the dustbin, it will get stolen by aliens...the dog will be sick on it...your mum will use it for cat litter. None of these true but terrible events will ever be believed by teachers.

Ooooo!! ...Goooo...!! I do feel ....ill...!! Hooooo...

Jest in fun: There's something I can do that my teacher can never do.

What's that? . Read my writing.

Satchel full of hours of immaculately done homework

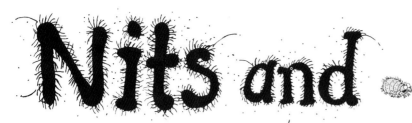

Nits and

Nits (head lice)

Nits are like a plague; like locusts, only smaller. Millions and millions of tiny creepy-crawlies suddenly live in your hair and crawl around on top of your head, making you really itch and scratch. If one kid in a school get nits then all the kids get nits, because nits can jump and breed very quickly.

Wot you lookin' at?

A close up of a nit (not life size)

Nits

Wow!

What do you call a teacher who has spots? Dot.

Nit Notes

1. Even teachers can get nits.

2. Teachers that are always finding fault with you are called nit-pickers.

3. A nit is also a dim-witted kid.

A nit comb or "bug rake"

Sometimes the "Nit Nurse" comes to school to see if any kids have nits. She uses a Nit Comb that really scratches your head.

Nurse or "Nursey"

Nice lady who gives out medicine tablets and pills when you are ill or when the Maths teacher has given you a headache. Puts ointment and plasters on playground bashings. But be warned – also tells porkie pies, especially about castor oil, syrup of figs and injections.

Oh, yeah!

This won't hurt

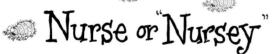

Zits

Old Mr Kelly
Had a pimple on his belly,
His wife cut it off,
And it tasted like jelly!

A close-up of a zit,
Possibly life-size.

Teachers will avoid the pitted and zitted as spontaneous eruptions can occur.

Zits are spots, boils, pimples, pustules* or blackheads. Blackheads are horrible blackheaded plugs of greasy gunge blocking up pores of skin on the face or neck. Boils are painful, pus-filled swellings. Pimples are smaller than boils.

*Pustule is an old word for pimple.

Abscess

'Orrible pustulant swelling, like a boil or zit, but much worse.

Zit Popping!

Ooze a lovely boil, then.

1. Finger Prod

2. Finger and Thumb Method

3. Two Finger Press

Great zits!

Thanks Babe

Spot Check
1. Spot on = exactly correct
2. Tight spot = difficult situation
3. High spot = best
4. In a spot = in trouble

School Kids Proverb
A watched boil never bursts.

Mind your Manners (dirty habits)

Manners

Manners are how teachers behave. At lunchtime, instead of the headmaster saying to the English teacher, "Hey! Fish-face! Gimme the ketchup!" he would say, "Excuse me, Miss Trout, would you be so kind as to pass me the ketchup? Thank you."

Recommended Reading: Gone with the Wind. Wind in the Willows.

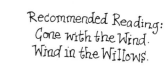

Belching or Burping

This is the noise kids make when they drink very quickly, open their mouths and go Burp! Kids think this is really funny.

(Warning: Teachers hate it.)

BURP!

BURP!

Gas Gag: Did you know that when the Queen belches she issues a royal pardon.

Bogey

A piece of dried snot bunged up your nose.

Nose Picker's Poem

Pick it, lick it.
Roll it, flick it.

Fire!

Nose-picking

Snot can be rooted out by a finger or politely blown into a tissue. Most kids pick the finger method. Kids with big nostrils can use their thumb.

Potty Posers:
Do you clean your top teeth with a toothbrush?
Yes.
What do you clean your bottom with

How do you stop your nose from running
Stick out your foot and trip it up.

A Phew Nasty Niffs

*Bogs (Toilets)

School loos are the smelliest place in school, but the most peaceful (a good place to think). Also a hang-out for stupid kids who smoke.

Smells are common in schools. The smell and stink of cabbage, cloakrooms, armpits, B.O. (Body Odours), bad breath, bogs*, cheesey feet and wind.

Pooh!

Why is a sausage rude? Because it spits.

Flatulence

A gassy explosion of wind from your bum (a bottom burp). Everybody has wind, even headmasters. Some are silent, some are mega loud and some are deadly poisonous. All kids are brill at it.

Bum

Kid's word for bottom.

Dirty Ditties

Inky, pinky, pen and inky.
I smell a dirty stinky.

NEVER
1. Spit
2. Gob
3. Drool
4. Dribble
5. Snigger
6. Sneer
7. Smirk (at teacher)

A snotty nosed kid is either a kid who is stuck-up (posh) or someone with a runny nose.

green snot candles

Sleeve Wipe

You can get rid of your snotty nose by using toilet paper, a handkerchief, tissues, or the back of your sleeve. But it's bad manners to lick it in public.

* **Snot**: also a term of abuse ie. Don't get snotty with me or You little snot!

Infections and Afflictions...

Infections

Lots of kids come to school with horrible pestilent infections like measles or mumps or bubonic plague and infect all the other kids and the teachers. (see also Germs) (see also Sneezes)

GET AWAY FROM ME!

Mumps

Rotten painful disease. Glands in neck swell up really big. Makes victim look like a hamster. (Warning: keep well away from anyone who looks like a hamster.)

I don't feel well

Measles

Very spotty disease. Like bubonic plague it's "dead" infectious. (see Germs)

Germs

Tiny titchy little creatures that you can't see but they are all over school and everywhere, especially on dirty hands, dogs' breath, dogs' poo and flies' feet.

Faint

Woozy, dizzy feeling where you conk out in exams when you haven't the faintest idea what the answers are. Also a good wheeze for getting out of lessons.

Vomit (School lunch re-run)

Contents of stomach ejected through mouth. Warning signs of somebody about to vomit:* green sweaty face, shaking shoulders and moaning. Get out of the way quickly! Very messy!

Ooooo

* Kids can feel sick at exam time.

Dangers and Diseases

Teacher's Sick Joke:
Why did Smith swallow 50p, Sir?
It was his dinner money.

What's a sick joke, Teacher?
Something you mustn't bring
up in the conversation.

SNIFF!
SNIFF!

Here's your coffee, Sir.

Sneezes
Another major irritation for teachers, especially
children who sneeze germs all over them.

Teachers hate kids
with coughs and colds,
especially really drippy kids.

TISHOO!

Sick note: Letter for Teacher
when you have been sick.

MORE SICK NOTES
Warts
Lumpy growths on hands or face.

Worms
Revolting, horrible plague of
little worms that live inside you.
Gross! Yuk! Your dog can also get
worms. Give him a worm tablet.

FOOT NOTE
Fungus
Some feet get fungus growing on them,
especially between the toes. This is called
athlete's foot (a good reason not to be an
athlete). Some teachers are known as
fungus face, but this is not athlete's face.

Verruca
These are painful warts on the foot or
hand. Brill excuse for getting off games.

Vesuvius

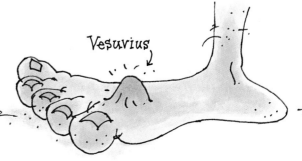

Teachers

Types and Traits

A teacher needs to be brainy, brawny and brave.

All-Seeing Teacher

It is well known that some teachers have eyes in the back of their heads, *SO BE CAREFUL.*

"I told you to get a haircut yet," said the teacher. "I did, sir. That one."

> Take that gum out of your mouth, Jenkins

Pupil's Proverb

What the eye doesn't see, the teacher doesn't grieve over.

Why did the teacher have to wear sunglasses?
Because her pupils were so bright.

> I've got my eye on you.

Transfixed with terror

Pupil Power

It is also a fact that some teachers have one eye bigger than the other. This is why they are always saying, "I've got my eye on you". (Take a good look at your teacher and work out which eye is the biggest.)

Eye-openers
- I don't believe my eyes.
- I'm all eyes.
- Don't pull the wool over my
- I'm up to my eyes.
- This is eyewash.

School Proverb:
If a teacher asks you a question and you don't know the answer ~ mumble.

Highly-strung Teacher
(often Music Teacher)

These teachers need peace and quiet, so they will shout QUIET! a million times a day. Weird!

QUIET!

GASP!

GASP!

Teacher's motto ~ Silence is golden.

Overheard: Quiet, I said quiet. Can you hear me, quiet? Stop this riot, quiet. QUIET, I WANT QUIET!

Funny Teacher

Some teachers like telling jokes, really unfunny, really pathetic jokes. Try to laugh. If you can go hee! hee! when all the other kids go, what?? huh?? you will become teacher's pet. (see Teacher's Pet)

NB: Encourage your teacher to tell more jokes. Remember, more laughs, less lesson.

Pounds, shillings, pence.
Teacher has no sense.
She came to school
To act the fool.
Pounds, shillings, pence.

... and to get to the other side Ha! Ha!

Hee! Hee!

Warning
Beyond a joke means **no** longer funny.

You must be joking means I do **not** believe you.

It's no joke means it is now **serious**

"Sir, my pen scratches."
"Perhaps it's got an itch."

Teacher's Tickler
Stop scratching your head, aren't you afraid of splinters?

Chalk and . . .

Has anyone seen 2B or not 2B?

Tense Teacher

By the end of term many teachers have reached the end of their tether and are ready to blow their top. Beware! The danger signs to watch out for are pencil snapping, throwing chalk, twitching violently and foaming at the mouth.

TWITCH

TWITCHY

SNAP!

I'm off!

Why did that school kid take h bike to school?

She wanted to drive her teache up the wall.

Why did Henry VIII have so many wives? Because he liked to chop and change.

Mad Teacher
(The Ranter)

These teachers are a classical type. They generally teach Latin and Greek. These are dead languages and Latin teachers can be old and fossilized with age. Your feeble efforts at Latin verbs are enough to set them ranting and raving. Latin is mostly about Caesar and his long wars. Most kids do not understand Greek. That's why they often say, "It's all Greek to me."

DANGER SIGNS
i) Hair stands on end.
ii) Bulging eyes.

God's teeth! Whose book is **this**?

Hunch caused by correcting exercise books

Latin Laughs

What was the Roman's greatest achievement?

Learning Latin, Sir.

Latin is a dead language,
As dead as dead can be,
First it killed the Romans,
Now it's killing me!

Mutinous Muttering
Sir is kind and Sir is gentle,
Sir is strong and
Sir is mental.

BEWARE:
Hell hath no fury li
a teacher scorned.

Talk

> I...HAVE...
> TOLD...YOU...
> AND...TOLD...
> ...YOU...
> UNTIL...
> I...AM...BLUE
> ...IN...THE
> ...FACE!

Dictator

These teachers are very bossy, tyrannical and despotic. They want their own way all the time. Avoid these teachers as they are mega-dangerous. Danger signs to watch for: bulging eyes, red cheeks, dribbling lips and quivering jowls, and speaking very slowly in CAPITAL LETTERS (SLOWSPEAK).

EEK!

Jabbing pointy finger

Natter Notes
- Idle talk
- Talk through the back of your head.
- Speak when you're spoken to.
- That will teach you a lesson.

Teacher Trivia
When lady teachers went to school, they wore big knickers so they could tuck their skirts into them for games.

Teacher Talk
(Mad Maxims) →

Teachers must have good communication skills to get through to the thick-headed, halfwitted and gormless. Here are some typical teacher sayings. Can you think of any more?

> Every time I open my mouth, some idiot starts talking.
> If you shout, I cannot hear you.
> There are no dull subjects, only dull pupils.
> You will not find the answer on the ceiling.
> If you run, you will not get there any faster.
> If you wish to talk, you must ask me first.
> If you do not come back, I will not let you go again.
> Let me give you a piece of my mind.
> * This will hurt me more than it will hurt you. (see Cane)

Touchy Teacher

Some teachers can become irritable and bad tempered, especially when marking exercise books and writing reports. Do not disturb. When they say YESSS? they mean what do you want, and why are you bothering me, you little pest.

Quick Quip
Please, Sir, May I leave the room?
Well you can't take it with you.

YESSSSSSS?!

* Said to author during painstaking research while still at school.

Oh! dear, what can the matter be?
Old Miss Bilge is locked in the laboratory.
She'll be there from Monday to Saturday.
Nobody cares that she's there.

> Get off! You little ** ?!

Biology Teacher

These teachers are agile and nimble. They flit around the classroom teaching about birds, bees, things that swim, and rabbits. They love nature and all living creatures, especially small furry things and worms.

> It likes you, Miss.

What kind of food do pelicans eat?
Anything that fits the bill, Miss.

> Was that meant to happen Sir?

Chemistry Teacher

These teachers love to experiment. They are practical and good with their hands. But they will insist on telling kids the same thing over and over and <u>over</u> again.

> How many times, Jeckyll, have I told you **not** to drink that stuff?

Physics Teacher

These teachers often blow up when they least expect it. They can be nervous.

important Chemistry lesson, Sally?
Never to lick the spoon, Sir.

History is a mystery.

History Teacher

Some History teachers have very big ears. This means they have incredibly good hearing. Always whisper within 50 metres of any History teachers.

More History Hoots

Please Sir, I wish we lived in the olden days.
Why?
Then there wouldn't be so much history to learn.

History Howler

Can anyone tell me what Gandhi's first name was?
Goosie, Goosie.

Where did Napoleon keep his armies?
Up his sleevies.

I heard that, Jones.

Silly old fool.

Which King of England invented the fireplace?
Alfred the Grate.

?**!GUM!

Tennis Elbow

A good sport

Games Teacher

Games teachers hate kids who forget their games kit. They will also seethe with rage at the sight of a sick note. They are very fit, healthy teachers who do not understand the sickly, weedy or wimpy. They rarely, if ever, take off their old tracksuits and smelly trainers. (Can suffer from athlete's foot.) Games lessons are also known as P.T. (Physical Torture), or P.E. (Physical Extermination).

N.B. Gum Warning: All teachers really hate chewing and bubble gum. They go absolutely bonkers if they tread or sit in it.

Why is the school football pitch always wet?
Because the kids are always dribbling.

Tip: Do not mention frogs or French tarts. They do not like it.

French Teacher

French teachers always speak French. This can be irritating. They do not listen unless you also speak French in class. Do not worry, add an occasional le, la or vous and you will get by.

Sacre bleu!

Miss! Miss!

Where am I? Where should I be?

Supply Teacher

These teachers are always coming and going. They never stay long enough to know your name, if you have homework to do, or what time of the day it is.

FRANGLAIS
le weekend
le T.V.
le telephone
le hamburger

What do French school kids say at the end of their school dinner? Merci.

Did you hear about the teacher who kept his wife under the bed? He thinks she's a little potty.

Understanding Teachers

This is difficult. Only swots, cleverdicks and brainy kids understand what teachers are saying.

Huh!

I know, I know!

I don't.

A Silly Sonnet

I haven't a clue,
I wish I knew.
My brain is aching.
My eyes are sore.
Oh, what is all this learning for?

Top Tip: Always put your hand up, even if you don't know the answer. Teachers will always ask kids who don't put up their hands. (see Hands

Maths Teacher

Maths teachers can be mean and moody. This is because Maths can give you a headache. To keep a Maths teacher happy, look keen and interested in class, even if you are clueless. Maths teachers are good at Mental Arithmetic. They say things like, "Is that the sum total of your homework?"

NB: Buy a calculator. Know your Tables.

Why are some fractions rude?
Because they're vulgar.

Maths Mirth
What is a polygon?
A dead parrot.

... I was attacked by a wild bear on the bus, Sir. And it ate all my homework.

Well... What is it **this** time, Craig?

N.B. Teachers rarely - if ever - believe excuses about late or lost homework.

The Head

(Skull, bonce, brain-case, boss, Master.)

A creature that rises from the grave to drink the blood of the living and prey mercilessly on others. Preys on the unwary. Not often seen in daylight.

Warning: Avoid being sent to visit the Head.*

Ghastly Giggle:
What do you call a teacher with a bus on his head?
Dead.

I'm ready for **you** now.

Headspeak:
Heads will roll.

Headmaster: "Boy, you should have been here an hour ago."
Boy: "Why, what happened?"

It's for my Gran, Sir.

C.D.T. Teacher
(Completely Daft Technology)

These teachers can help you to design and make things. They usually have a tool in hand and are known by the nickname "Chips". They like making stools.

* Not to be confused with head (loo) on boats (Ed.)

Gym Mistress

Jolly, sporty type who organises outdoor games like Hockey and Netball. They make kids skip, hop, stretch, vault, run on the spot, and jog until they drop. Avoid – they are dangerously hyperactive. Will go white water rafting, potholing, and bungy jumping in their hols.

Net!

Greedy Gag:

There once was a schoolboy called kid
Who ate 20 pies for a quid.
When asked, "Are you faint?"
He replied, "No I ain't.
But I don't feel as well as I did!"

Hockey
Game played with a stick and a bully. (See Bully)

Netball
Really soppy boring game where you have to jump around and put a ball in a net 20 ft off the ground. The only people who like netball are the fit healthy kids with long arms.

Foul Food
Please Miss, can I lick the bowl?
No, Sharon, flush it like the other kids.

It's toad in the hole, Miss.

Domestic Science Teacher

These teachers teach kids how and what to cook. They are extremely clean and like their food. Cooking is a bit like a Chemistry lesson. You mix and stir things together, put them in the oven and stand well back.

With real toads

Our teacher went on a special banana diet. Did she lose weight? No, but she couldn't half climb trees.

Domestic Science teachers' favourite recipes are: Toad in the Hole, Shepherd's Pie, Rock cakes, Bath Buns, Jam Roly Poly and Swiss Roll.

School Dinners

It's yummy.

After a hard morning of learning, kids need to eat. Some kids bring packed lunches: some have school dinners. Dinners at school can be really brill or seriously 'orrible. If the dinner ladies think you're sweet and need "fattening up", you could get hamburgers and chips, sausage and chips, curry and chips, or fish and chips every day. But if the dinner ladies think you're a real slob, you will get cabbage, cabbage and cabbage.

School dinners make you sicker quicker.

Dinner Ladies

Probably the most important people in school. Never, never cheek a dinner lady. Kids can get thin if they upset the dinner ladies. They can also get more than their fair share of cabbage (yuk!)

Cabbage

Green, smelly and disgusting. Teachers had to eat lots and lots of this when they were kids.

I feel sick

I eat peas with honey.
I've done it all my life
It makes the peas taste funny
But it keeps them on the knife.

Yuk!

Rotten Rhymes

Don't eat school Dinners
Just throw them aside,
A lot of kids didn't, a lot of kids died.

The meat's made of iron,
The spuds are of steel.
And if they don't kill,
the pudding will!

Custard

Lumpy, yellow school pudding. Chew well before eating or swallowing.

Tortures

School can be torture but long ago it was really gruesome. Kids got bashed, birched, caned, clouted, larruped, lashed, slapped, slippered, smacked and strapped.

Cane

This popular instrument of torture was used by cruel teachers in ancient olden days (before colour TV was invented).

WALLOPER'S WIT
Spare the rod and spoil the child.
You've got to be cruel to be kind.

Cretin's Corner

Putting kids in the corner kept them quiet.

Teachers often ruled by the ruler

Rulers made a handy weapon for wicked teachers to rap the dim on the knuckles. (Very painful.)

The traditional Lughole pinch, twist and pull

Any kids who upset teachers were liable to be dragged out by an ear. The result of this cruel torture could be why so many old people have big ears. Check out Granny and Grandad's lugs.

When do you like school most?
At weekends, holidays and when I'm off sick.

Cruel Crack
Why did so many kids go to the Headmaster's funeral?
To make sure he was really dead

S'not fair!

Pay attention to avoid detention.

Detention

Terrible punishment invented by cruel teachers – victim is imprisoned in classroom during break or after school hours.

Reports

Reports are the sneaky things that teachers write about kids to their parents. They make up lots of "porky pies" in order to get kids into trouble.

Lines

Rotten punishment given by cruel teachers where you get blistered fingers writing the same thing over and...over and...over and... over and...over and...over...again.

Test Teasers

What exams do farmers take?
Hay Levels.

How do R.E. Teachers mark exams?
With Spirit Levels.

When I'm lying cold and dead.
Put my school books by my head.
Tell Teacher I've got to rest.
And won't be back for the English Test.

What is my name?

How are you getting on with your exams?
Not bad, the questions are easy – it's the answers I have difficulty with.

Exams

Form of cruel torture. Exams are a test of what you have learnt. Or, more accurately, what you can remember of what you have learnt. They always begin with "write your name at the top of the page".

Expel

If you do something really bad at school, like forget your homework twice in one week, you could be expelled or turfed out of school and never, never, never be allowed back in. (Wow!)

Side-Splitters: I hope I didn't see you looking at Tom's work?
I hope you didn't either, Sir.

Teacher's Prayer

One more day of sin.
One more day of sorrow.
One more day in
this old dump
And we stay at home
tomorrow.

Thank goodness for that!